MANNA FROM HEAVEN

21 DAYS OF NOURISHMENT
FOR THE SOUL

CJ HITZ

Manna from Heaven: 21 Days of Nourishment for the Soul
By CJ Hitz
Published by Body and Soul Publishing LLC
Colorado Springs, CO 80904
© 2021 CJ Hitz

ISBN 978-1-946118-21-9

Day 20 "This is not my Home" used with permission by Kim Bookmyer

CONTENTS

INTRODUCTION

If you've ever experienced seasons of financial difficulty where it was a struggle to simply put food on the table, imagine how Moses must have felt after he and his fellow Israelites fled Egypt and now found themselves in the wilderness.

We know there were about 600,000 men not counting the women and children (Exodus 12:37). A very conservative estimate could easily be over 2 million mouths to feed! And it didn't take long for Moses to begin hearing groans from both bellies and mouths. Talk about a stressful situation!

Thankfully, Moses wouldn't need to "whip anything up" for a dinner party of over 2 million. Instead, the same God who miraculously delivered His people from the clutches of Pharoah, would now supernaturally provide food from the very storehouses of heaven.

"The Israelites called the food manna. It was white like coriander seed, and it tasted like honey wafers." (Exodus 16:31 NLT)

The Hebrew word for manna literally means, "What is it?"

What would start off as a fresh dew would evaporate and turn into "a flaky substance as fine as frost blanketing the ground." (16:14)

And there you have it! The first documented instance of people having Mountain Dew and Frosted Flakes for breakfast. Just kidding of course :-)

God would provide this heavenly food day in and day out for forty years! (16:35)

The Psalmist puts it this way as he recalls this incredible period in Israel's history,

"He rained down manna for them to eat; he gave them bread from heaven. They ate the food of angels! God gave them all they could hold." (Psalm 78:24-25)

Over the course of these next twenty-one days, it's my hope that God would supply spiritual manna from heaven for our souls. Each day is meant to provide some nourishment from the endless feast that is God's Word.

These days might also feel like little appetizers that whet your appetite to dig into the Bible even more. Most of all, I pray that we would encounter the true Manna from heaven found in Christ,

"Jesus replied, "I am the bread of life. Whoever comes to me will never be hungry again. Whoever believes in me will never be thirsty." (John 6:35)

With open hands and humble hearts, we pray, "Father, give us today our daily bread."

DAY 1
Secret Stash

Meanwhile, the disciples were urging Jesus, "Rabbi, eat something." But Jesus replied, "I have a kind of food you know nothing about." – John 4:31-32 (NLT)

After I took up running in my mid-thirties, I would eventually lose over fifty pounds in the course of several years. On one particular trip to Oregon to visit my family, I'll never forget the horrified looks on the faces of my mom and grandma as they saw my "malnourished" running frame.

"Are you ok?", they nervously asked. "I haven't felt better in years!", I responded.

Still not convinced, they proceeded to dump some of their Mexican meal onto my already full plate while saying emphatically, "We need to put some meat on your bones!"

I can just imagine the disciples trying to force-feed Jesus after returning with some grub. Who wouldn't be hungry (and thirsty) after a forty mile dusty walk from Jerusalem? We runners would refer to this little jaunt as an "ultramarathon." You're going to be famished whether you're walking or running this distance.

Upon reaching this Samaritan village of Sychar, we read these words,

"Jesus, tired from the long walk, sat wearily beside the well about noontime." (John 4:6)

The worn-out and parched Rabbi the disciples had left in search of food now seemed to be as fresh as a daisy upon their return.

Jesus had a secret stash of food nobody else knew about,

"My nourishment comes from doing the will of God, who sent me, and from finishing his work." (John 4:34)

Though physically fatigued, Jesus gave what he had in order to satisfy the spiritual hunger and thirst of a Samaritan woman weighed down with shame. In the process, Jesus felt refreshed.

There's something rejuvenating about doing what God has called us to do, even when we're weary from life's "long walks."

Reflection: Recall the times in your life when you felt nourished and energized after doing the will of God. What work is God calling you to finish today?

DAY 2
Heart and Soul

*"Do all that you have in mind," his armor-bearer said.
"Go ahead; I am with you heart and soul."*
– 1 Samuel 14:7 (NIV)

One of my favorite stories in the bible is found in 1 Samuel 14:1-23 and involves one of my favorite individuals from scripture named Jonathan. He's certainly the named hero of the story and the guy who initiates a daring plan. It's his bright idea to go and pick a fight with the Philistines without telling his dad who just happens to be the king.

Jonathan was tired of waiting around in the shade while an enemy army was wreaking havoc all around them. He would rather stand up and risk his life than to remain sitting (or snoozing) in temporary security.

There's another guy who was apparently tired of twiddling his thumbs as well. We don't know his name but we know his title of armor bearer.

Armor bearers were servants who carried extra weapons for commanders. They were also responsible for finishing off enemies their commander had wounded on the battlefield along with being the eyes and ears protecting their master from behind.

After Jonathan laid out his crazy scheme, we can feel the depth of loyalty in the armor bearer's response,

"Go ahead; I am with you heart and soul."

In other words, "I've got your back no matter what."

When I was a Campus Life Director in an organization called Youth For Christ, I had my own "armor bearer" who was one of the most devoted and humble volunteers I've ever known. From setting up chairs for our weekly meetings to cleaning up the messes left by teenagers we ministered to, Craig was with me 'heart and soul.'

Week after week and month after month, Craig showed up with a willingness to carry out any unglamorous task that was asked of him. I'm grateful I had the opportunity to serve alongside this quiet warrior who always had my back.

The armor bearers in life may not receive much glory and recognition, but their value is priceless. Just ask Jonathan.

Reflection: Take a moment to write out a list of the "armor bearers" you've had in your corner. Who can you be an armor bearer for?

DAY 3
Power in Weakness

"Three different times I begged the Lord to take it away. Each time he said, "My grace is all you need. My power works best in weakness." So now I am glad to boast about my weaknesses, so that the power of Christ can work through me." – 2 Corinthians 12:8-9 (NLT)

Though you might not be familiar with the name Nicolas Herman, you might know the name Brother Lawrence who served in a Carmelite monastery in Paris, France during the 1600s.

This humble, lay brother was made popular by the little book, *The Practice of the Presence of God*, which was compiled after his death and contains writings from some of the letters he sent. Brother Lawrence was known for the intimacy he expressed with God but he was also known for his physical weakness.

Having been injured to the point of being lame, the simplest tasks became difficult including traveling to Burgundy to buy the provision of wine for the monastery. On many occasions, he could hardly remember how the task was accomplished except God helped him moment by moment.

Brother Lawrence gives us a picture of almost pathetic weakness and dependence during his fifty years as a cook and dishwasher for the monastery. He was known as a "Great awkward fellow who broke everything."

But even with his many shortcomings, it was said that, "He accustomed himself to do everything for the love of God, and with prayer, upon all occasions, for His grace to do his work well."

Whether it's Paul the Apostle or Brother Lawrence, it seems that God does His best work through our weaknesses in order to drive us to Himself. Our weaknesses are meant to create a dependence upon Him alone. I believe God will even spend decades cultivating weakness in our lives.

In the words of Brother Lawrence, "The higher perfection a soul aspires after, the more dependent it is upon Divine Grace."

Reflection: In a world that tries to eliminate weakness, how has God been glorified through some of your own weaknesses? Write out a list of accomplishments you know wouldn't have happened without God's strength.

DAY 4
Try Tears

"My heart is filled with bitter sorrow and unending grief for my people, my Jewish brothers and sisters. I would be willing to be forever cursed—cut off from Christ!—if that would save them." – Romans 9:2-3 (NLT)

In the 1920s, a group of Salvation Army soldiers were sent into the ghettos of Los Angeles in order to bring the hope of the Gospel to hurting people. After three years of laboring with little to no results, this discouraged team sent a telegram to their Salvation Army founder, General William Booth,

"It just won't work. We have tried everything. The Gospel is just not being received here."

A couple days later they received the following two word telegram from General Booth,

"Try Tears."

Do we ache inside to the point of tears for those around us? We can almost feel the pain of the Apostle Paul as he writes these words with his tears, "My heart is filled with bitter sorrow and unending grief for my people…"

On numerous occasions throughout the gospels, we read that Jesus was filled with compassion for those around him. (Luke 7:13; Matthew 15:32; Matthew 9:36; Matthew 14:14; Matthew 20:34; Mark 8:2-3)

The word for compassion in Greek means "to be moved as to one's bowels." The intestines were thought to be the seat of love and pity. Jesus literally felt like his intestines were turning inside out for those he encountered. It was a deep anguish.

It's so easy to grow numb to the pain around us. We hear horrible things in the news without a second thought. If we're not careful, our hearts become hardened and callous toward things that break God's heart.

I'm ashamed to say that my eyes have become dry on many occasions. When I'm not close to the heartbeat of Jesus, a spiritual drought begins to slowly dry up my soul. Eventually, the Lord will gently tug at my heartstrings through something or someone and warm tears begin filling dry riverbeds.

It's good to cry. May we not be ashamed to ask for more tears in our lives.

Reflection: If you've felt dry, lift up this prayer, "Father, I ask that you break my heart with the things that break Yours. Stamp eternity on my eyes and give me tears for those who are hurting all around me. In Jesus' name I pray, Amen."

DAY 5
Over My Dead Body

"There is one God and one Mediator who can reconcile
God and humanity—the man Christ Jesus. He gave his life
to purchase freedom for everyone."
– 1 Timothy 2:5-6a (NLT)

Most of us are familiar with the phrase, "Over my dead body." When we're emphatic about preventing something from happening, we use these words for emphasis. A couple of examples might include,

"If my neighbor goes ahead with his plan to cut down this tree, he'll have to do so over my dead body."

"You think I'm going to give you the keys to my car? Over my dead body!"

If anyone throughout history has ever gone out of their way to prevent something from happening, it was the Son of God. By taking on flesh and ultimately dying for the sin of mankind, Jesus essentially said,

"If you insist on spending eternity in hell, you're going to have to step over my dead (and risen) body to do so."

I've heard some ask, "How can a loving God send people to a place of eternal torment?"

I think an even better question is, "How can people reject such an incredible offer of salvation by refusing the greatest gift ever given?"

As 1 Timothy 2:6a says, "He (Jesus) gave his life to purchase freedom for everyone."

Did you catch that last part? The payment made by Jesus on a bloody Roman cross over 2000 years ago was enough for anyone and everyone to get in on this eternal freedom!

Rather than God sending people to hell, He did everything possible to prevent people from ending up in a place originally created for the devil and his angels. (Matthew 25:41)

As those who have been saved, we now have the privilege and responsibility of pleading with others to avoid an eternity apart from God. As preacher Charles Spurgeon used to say, "If sinners be damned, at least let them leap to hell over our dead bodies."

Reflection: How does it feel to know that God gave His very best to secure your freedom? Who needs to hear the words, "Over my dead body," from you today?

DAY 6
A Walk in The Dark

"Who among you fears the LORD and obeys his servant?
If you are walking in darkness, without a ray of light, trust
in the LORD and rely on your God."
– Isaiah 50:10 (NLT)

Ask anyone who's ever run a 100 mile trail race in the wilderness to share some advice and most of them will tell you to 1.) Expect to run long stretches by yourself and 2.) Get used to running in the dark with only the rays of your headlamp lighting the trail ahead. After all, these races take most runners 24 hours or more to finish!

In many ways, this is good advice for the Christian life. If you've been walking with the Lord long enough, you know there are those seasons that seem as if we're wandering in a wilderness all alone under the cover of darkness.

Whether it's spiritual dryness, the loss of a loved one, or the diagnosis of a life-threatening illness, we're bound to experience what St. John of the Cross called, "The Dark Night of the Soul."

Consider some others who experienced their own times of darkness and loneliness,

Abraham - "As the sun was going down, Abram fell into a deep sleep, and a terrifying darkness came down over him." (Genesis 15:12)

Psalmist - "You have taken away my companions and loved ones. Darkness is my closest friend." (Psalm 88:18)

Job – Read Job chapter 3, one of the darkest chapters in scripture.

Hagar – "So Abraham got up early the next morning, prepared food and a container of water, and strapped them on Hagar's shoulders. Then he sent her away with their son, and she wandered aimlessly in the wilderness of Beersheba." (Genesis 21:14)

Jesus – "At noon, darkness fell across the whole land until three o'clock. Then at three o'clock Jesus called out with a loud voice, "Eloi, Eloi, lema sabachthani?" which means "My God, my God, why have you abandoned me?"

Thankfully, even when we might feel like we're alone, there is Someone who never leaves or forsakes us (Deuteronomy 31:6; Hebrews 13:5; Psalm 23:4).

A walk (or run) in the dark is not a walk in the park, but it's in these times when we come to 'trust the Lord and rely on our God' even more.

Reflection: Recall a "dark night of the soul" you endured and how the Lord brought you through it. Ponder the following quote by St. John of the Cross: "In the dark night of the soul, bright flows the river of God."

DAY 7
Sound Asleep

*"Then he returned to the disciples and found them asleep.
He said to Peter, "Couldn't you watch with me even one
hour?" – Matthew 26:40 (NLT)*

My wife Shelley and I have often joked that she has
the "spiritual gift of sleep." While it takes her seconds
to fall into deep sleep after her head hits the pillow, it
often takes me minutes (or hours) to be in dreamland.

Years ago there was a house directly across the street
from ours that caught fire in the middle of the night
(thankfully, no one was hurt). Even with the flashing
lights and sirens of two fire trucks, five police cars,
and our barking dog, my bride was oblivious to the
commotion right outside the window she slept beside.

Sound asleep.

Could it be that many of us in the Church have been
snoozing while trouble swirls all around us? I've been
walking with Jesus for nearly thirty years, yet there
have been periods of "sleep walking" mixed in. I'm

afraid it took a worldwide pandemic to help wake me up from my own slumber.

Since the beginning of 2020, it seems as if the sirens have been getting louder with each passing month. In a world coming apart at the seams, I've distinctly heard the Lord saying, "Wake up CJ, I need you to watch with me in this last hour…I need you to be alert."

Paul's words to the Romans couldn't be any more relevant today,

"This is all the more urgent, for you know how late it is; time is running out. Wake up, for our salvation is nearer now than when we first believed. The night is almost gone; the day of salvation will soon be here." (Romans 13:11-12a)

Emerge (to rise from) + Urgency (requiring swift action) = emergency

We're living in a spiritual state of emergency like we've never seen. We believers in Christ are like the emergency personnel who sacrifice sleep in order to attend to those in greatest need.

Open up, open up
And give yourself away
Ya see the need, ya hear the cries
So how can you delay?
The world is sleeping in the dark

That the church just can't fight
'Cause it's asleep in the light

From the song "Asleep In The Light" by the late Keith Green

Reflection: Ask the Lord to show you specific areas that you've been sound asleep in and write them down. "Father, awaken me from my slumber and use me as one of your spiritual first responders."

DAY 8
Downtime

Then Jesus said, "Let's go off by ourselves to a quiet place and rest awhile." – Mark 6:31a (NLT)

During the summers while I was in college, I worked in a large sawmill that produced various sizes of lumber (i.e. 2x4, 2x6, 4x4, etc.). Each week, the sawmill would completely shut down for a couple shifts in order to perform regular maintenance. It was this downtime that allowed the normal working shifts to operate smoothly and be most productive.

Webster's gives us the following definition for the word downtime,

"Time during which production is stopped especially during setup for an operation or when making repairs."

In a world that values productivity even if it means burning out, it's good to know that Jesus is a firm believer in taking downtime. We see a clear example of this in Mark 6 after Jesus sends his twelve apostles out on a ministry trip.

Mark 6:30 says, "The apostles returned to Jesus from their ministry tour and told him all they had done and taught."

With the authority of their Master, these guys were teaching, preaching, anointing, praying, and casting (out demons). Things were happening. Momentum was building. Crowds were growing. Time to strike while the iron's hot! Is Jesus going to expand the world tour? Not exactly.

"Then Jesus said, "Let's go off by ourselves to a quiet place and rest awhile." He said this because there were so many people coming and going that Jesus and his apostles didn't even have time to eat." (Mark 6:31)

In other words, "Let's take a little vacation in order to recharge our batteries."

This getaway after an exhausting ministry trip would allow them to refuel physically, emotionally, and spiritually. Rather than halting progress, this downtime would allow the team to be even more fruitful and focused.

When the Creator of the universe invites you to rest, don't hesitate to take Him up on it.

Reflection: Have you ever been so busy you didn't even have time to eat? Schedule some downtime where you truly rest from your labors and allow God to recharge your batteries.

DAY 9
Into The Depths

"For he has rescued us from the kingdom of darkness and transferred us into the Kingdom of his dear Son, who purchased our freedom and forgave our sins."
– Colossians 1:13-14 (NLT)

In his classic book, Miracles, author C.S. Lewis gives us a wonderful illustration of Christ representing a pearl diver in search of hidden treasure. It's a beautiful passage that your own eyes should read,

"One may think of a diver, first reducing himself to nakedness, then glancing in mid-air, then gone with a splash, vanishing rushing down through green and warm water into black and cold water, down through increasing pressure into the deathlike region of ooze and slime and old decay; then up again, back to colour and light, his lungs almost bursting, till suddenly he breaks the surface again, holding in his hand the dripping, precious thing he went down to recover. He and it are both coloured now that they have come up into the light: down below, where it lay colorless in the dark, he lost his color too." (Miracles, chap. 14).

Can you believe that you and I are that 'dripping, precious thing' Jesus went down to recover? If you're like me, it's a thought that seems beyond what my little finite mind can comprehend.

We've become quite comfortable here in our 'region of ooze and slime and old decay.' So comfortable that we forget that we were created for much more. The Son of God volunteered to descend into the depths of darkness in order to bring us into His glorious light.

Not only is this pearl diver the One who retrieves us, but his very life becomes the currency used in order to purchase us for display in the Father's kingdom collection.

I can imagine the great Pearl Diver regaling the angels in heaven with stories from some of his deep dives…

"I found this one in the depths of despair and depression."

"This beauty was pulled from the sea of drug & alcohol addiction."

"A shark tried to snatch this one away from me but I eventually got her to safety. Got a few scars to prove it but you should see the shark…at least what's left of him."

Perhaps even now the angels are on the edge of their seats hearing Him tell your story.

Reflection: How does it feel to know how valuable you are to the Pearl Diver and his Father? Share your story of going from the kingdom of darkness to the Kingdom of light.

DAY 10
No Longer Ashamed

"For I am not ashamed of this Good News about Christ. It is the power of God at work, saving everyone who believes—the Jew first and also the Gentile."
– Romans 1:16 (NLT)

Some experiences can be more memorable than others. My first at bat for the Myrtle Creek Hornets tee-ball team provided one such lasting memory. With a hefty swing that would've made Babe Ruth proud, I smacked a line drive up the middle and into center field. Half-shocked, I heard screams of, "Run!", from every direction.

I can just imagine the pride my mom and grandma must have felt as I began hustling toward first base. With the ball going through the center fielder's legs, could I possibly stretch this into a double?

Unfortunately, we'll never know. After stepping on first base, I followed that fresh line of chalk until it ended somewhere in right field. The possibility of a double evaporated into a definite out. Mom and grandma's initial pride soon turned into embarrassment as they tried to hide under the bleachers. Talk about a swing of emotions!

Thankfully, this memorable sports blooper has provided many laughs through the years. You'll be thrilled to know that my mom and grandma are no longer ashamed to be seen with me in public.

The emotions of feeling ashamed or embarrassed hit each of us at various points in life. We become embarrassed by our own actions or those of our family. We can also become ashamed or embarrassed to be seen with certain people. Craving the approval of others, we may go out of our way to avoid those who are looked down upon by society.

I'm ashamed to say that there have been moments in my life when I've felt ashamed of being associated with Jesus. Whether it's on an airplane or in a grocery store, how many opportunities to share Jesus have I missed?

On Sunday morning, we might boldly declare, like Peter, "Even if everyone else deserts you, I will never desert you." (Matthew 26:33). But on Monday morning, also like Peter, our lives proclaim, "I don't even know the man." (Matthew 26:72).

Like Peter, I'm so grateful for restoration and new opportunities to be associated with Jesus. If the Son of God disregarded the shame of the cross (Hebrews 12:2), I no longer need to be ashamed.

Reflection: Have you ever been ashamed or embarrassed to be seen with Jesus? Humbly come to Jesus and ask him to give you the boldness of Paul to "proclaim this Good News about Christ."

DAY 11
Suddenly

Jesus responded, "Why are you afraid? You have so little faith!" Then he got up and rebuked the wind and waves, and suddenly there was a great calm.
– Matthew 8:26 (NLT)

Live life long enough and you know how things can suddenly change with very little warning. Suddenly, we lose a loved one. Suddenly we're in a pandemic. Suddenly, I lost my job. Suddenly, our car broke down. Suddenly, our neighbor started yelling.

In early July of 2009, we received the sudden, unexpected news that Shelley's dad was assaulted near one of his rental properties. It took less than a minute for the damage to be done and Chuck would remain in a coma for nearly six weeks. Thankfully, he would eventually recover while still experiencing the lasting effects of a Traumatic Brain Injury.

Suddenly can change everything but what comes after that can vary. Here are a few examples of what happens when God is added to the equation,

"Suddenly, a fierce storm struck the lake, with waves breaking into the boat." (Matthew 8:24)

Uh oh, time to start panicking right? Hold your horses, let's see what happens a mere two verses later,

Jesus responded, "Why are you afraid? You have so little faith!" Then he got up and rebuked the wind and waves, and suddenly there was a great calm. (Matthew 8:26)

How about Paul and Silas being thrown into prison? It looked like the end of the road for this dynamic duo as they found themselves shackled in the inner dungeon (Acts 16:24). The bleak surroundings didn't prevent these guys from enjoying a time of prayer and worship (Acts 16:25). And then,

"Suddenly, there was a massive earthquake, and the prison was shaken to its foundations. All the doors immediately flew open, and the chains of every prisoner fell off!" (Acts 16:26)

This same Paul had been the ruthless Saul who was persecuting followers of Jesus throughout the region. "Saul was uttering threats with every breath and was eager to kill the Lord's followers." (Acts 9:1)

Just two verses later we read, "As he was approaching Damascus on this mission, a light from heaven suddenly shone down around him." (Acts 9:3)

As we place our trust in Jesus, it's comforting to know that He has the final say regarding what comes after our suddenly.

Reflection: How have you seen the Lord change a negative "suddenly" into a positive one for His glory? Call upon the Lord to have the final say regarding a recent "suddenly."

DAY 12
Homesick

"For this world is not our permanent home; we are looking forward to a home yet to come."
– Hebrews 13:14 (NLT)

For as long as I can remember, I've had a sense of adventure and wanderlust. Growing up in a small logging town in southern Oregon, I would imagine what it might be like to be transported to far off places. Perhaps this is why geography was one of my favorite subjects in school as maps could hold my attention for hours.

Looking back on my life, several examples of scratching that itch to explore come to mind:

- Fond memories of loading up the car for family road trips from Oregon to Wyoming.
- Traveling to Germany, Belgium and Holland for three weeks at age 17 to play with a basketball tour team.
- Choosing to attend a college 2,500 miles from home even though I had never visited the campus.

- Driving from Ohio to the country of Belize, Central America with my wife for a two year missionary journey early in our marriage.
- Several years of enjoying a speaking ministry that took me across the US and Canada.
- Traveling to the country of Slovenia to run in the World Masters Mountain Running Championship.

But one experience stands out above the others. Sometime in 2010, Shelley & I began discussing the possibility of traveling around the country in an RV. To be honest, this was my crazy idea (big surprise) and my very loving wife was willing to be supportive.

After emptying our house by selling or giving away a huge amount of our earthly possessions, we packed the bare essentials into a 1986 Toyota EZ-Ryder and hit the road in November of 2011. Three months later, we realized we'd had our fill of living and working in an aging 175 square foot leaky box on wheels.

What a trooper my wife was. Though she had a few doubts and questions about how this excursion might play out, she knew I needed to taste and see for myself.

Within six weeks, we laid down roots in the Rocky Mountains of Colorado and have called this place "home" ever since. The older I get, the more I appreciate being at home. The RV experience revealed something going on inside me in the form of discontent.

From the moment we're born, our wanderings point to a longing for our True Home. Still, we leave no stone unturned in trying to find an elusive heaven on earth.

As we allow Christ to make his home in our hearts (Ephesians 3:17), we find ourselves becoming more and more homesick for the place he's preparing for us.

There's just no place like home.

Reflection: Have you experienced cases of wanderlust in your life? "Father, as we become more uncomfortable in this world, give us a deeper longing for our True Home."

DAY 13
How Much More

"Consider the ravens: They do not sow or reap, they have no storeroom or barn; yet God feeds them. And how much more valuable you are than birds!" – Luke 12:24 (NIV)

We live in a world where fear and panic seem to be running loose like the bulls of Pamplona. We ask ourselves, "Will I make it through the streets without being stampeded or gored?"

News networks sell fear and panic by the truckload. There's a shortage of toilet paper. You'd better panic. Gas prices are rising. Time to worry. The water supply is diminishing. Let fear slowly take over. Meat is growing scarce. Better buy an extra freezer and stock up.

Though the pandemic has certainly turned up the fear, panic, worry and scarcity dials, the reality is that mankind has been dealing with these thorns throughout history. When Jesus came onto the scene two-thousand years ago, there was a worldwide 'pandemic' in the form of the brutal Roman Empire. Many were paralyzed by these same emotions.

What does the Messiah have to say about these weapons the enemy uses to try and take us down?

"Consider the ravens: They do not sow or reap, they have no storeroom or barn; yet God feeds them. And how much more valuable you are than birds!" (Luke 12:24)

How much more.

Have you ever seen a panicking bird stocking up on worms? Me either. Here in Colorado, we have an abundance of black-billed magpie birds. I enjoy watching them forage in the evenings in a field behind our house. They don't seem rushed or hurried as they're searching for food. It's like they're out for an evening stroll with a few pals as they soak up the last rays of sunlight. And then they do this the next day, and the next.

Unhurried, day to day living is what Jesus is getting at here.

Early in our marriage, Shelley and I experienced God's provision in a way that helped deepen our trust in Him. When I was working with Youth For Christ, I had to raise my full support in my first year. At the end of the first year, any amount above the $17,500 salary that came in would be split 50/50 between the office and myself.

With about a month left before I completed my first year at YFC, Shelley and I were doing our taxes and realized we had made a terrible miscalculation. Thinking at one time we would be getting a refund; we were horrified to find out we owed the IRS $2,500! Time to hit the panic button, right?

About two weeks before that payment was due, my Executive Director called me into his office to let me know I had just completed my first year and reminded me (I had forgotten) of their policy regarding funds coming in above my base salary.

Imagine my shock when he slid a check for $3,000 across his desk before saying, "You ended up with $6,000 that came in above your goal so here's the half we agreed to."

"And how much more valuable you are than birds!"

Reflection: Write down some of the ways you've experienced the Father's incredible provision through the years. Read Luke 12:22-34 and allow the words of Jesus to soak into your soul.

DAY 14
Permission Granted

"If anyone asks, 'What are you doing?' just say, 'The Lord needs it and will return it soon.'" – Mark 11:3 (NLT)

I'm trying to imagine the reaction I would get if I casually walked up to a bike rack on our local college campus and began taking one of the nicer bikes, only to have the owner or one of their friends witness this mischievous act. A reasonable response would certainly be, "What are you doing?"

My answer to that question could very well determine whether or not I spend a few nights in jail. Two disciples of Jesus found themselves in a similar suspicious act as they began untying a young donkey that didn't belong to them.

Jesus, knowing his partners in "crime" would get some pushback, gives them the secret password,

If anyone asks, 'What are you doing?' just say, 'The Lord needs it and will return it soon.'" (Mark 11:3)

Sure enough, the scenario plays out according to script,

"As they were untying it, some bystanders demanded, "What are you doing, untying that colt?" They said what Jesus had told them to say, and they were permitted to take it." (Mark 11:5-6)

I'm almost sure those two disciples had a case of the sweaty palms. After all, it was Palm Sunday (insert groan here). Any nervousness they might have been feeling quickly evaporated after they uttered the words, 'The Lord needs it and will return it soon.'

Those words were enough. No questions asked. Full permission was granted.

Would those words be enough for me? Does the Lord have full permission to come to my house and take whatever He needs without any further questions? Is there anything in my life that's off limits to the Lord? Do I have complete trust in the Son of God?

Little did the owner know that their donkey would be the one spoken of 500 years previous in a prophecy mentioned in Zechariah 9:9. We have no idea how the Lord will use the things we entrust to his care.

This story also reminds us that Jesus is the God of extraordinary detail. He goes before us to prepare the way. He has already thought of everything ahead of time and provides for our every need.

You can trust Jesus with your stuff.

Reflection: "If you help the poor, you are lending to the LORD—and he will repay you!" (Proverbs 19:17). What is it in your life that the Lord needs to borrow? Pray, "Jesus, I give you full permission to use anything in my life that will honor and glorify your name."

DAY 15
Eternal VacSINation

"Death is swallowed up in victory. O death, where is your victory? O death, where is your sting?"
– 1 Corinthians 15:55 (NLT)

Since the beginning of 2020, the world has been captivated by a specific virus. Though viruses have been around for thousands of years, the first evidence of the existence of viruses didn't occur until 1892.

But there's one virus that we know goes all the way back to a beautiful garden called Eden. From that first bite of forbidden fruit, this virus was unleashed upon the beautiful planet God created.

Out of the billions upon billions of humans who have ever walked upon earth, all but one has been infected with the sin virus which began spreading from our ancestors, Adam and Eve.

"When Adam sinned, sin entered the world. Adam's sin brought death, so death spread to everyone, for everyone sinned." (Romans 5:12 NLT)

This virus of sin was so potent that it took the Son of God taking on flesh in order to supply the necessary vaccine for humanity.

"For God made Christ, who never sinned, to be the offering for our sin, so that we could be made right with God through Christ." (2 Corinthians 5:21 NLT)

At best, every vaccine ever created in a lab has an expiration date. It's a temporary band aid. The most important decision you and I could ever make is to receive the only cure for the insidious viral infection running through our veins. An eternal vaccination that never expires!

Friends, if we're living in the last days (2 Timothy 3:1-5)—and we very well could be—have you been "vacSINated" by the shed blood of Jesus? (Hebrews 9:12)

It's as simple as ABC…

A – Admit you've sinned – "For everyone has sinned; we all fall short of God's glorious standard." (Romans 3:23 NLT)

B – Believe Jesus is Lord – "For the wages of sin is death, but the free gift of God is eternal life through Christ Jesus our Lord." (Romans 6:23 NLT)

C – Call upon His name – "If you openly declare that Jesus is Lord and believe in your heart that God raised him from the dead, you will be saved…For "Everyone who calls on the name of the LORD will be saved." (Romans 10:9, 13 NLT)

Reflection: Lift up this prayer from the depths of your heart - Jesus, I confess my need for the only cure found in You alone. I'm tired of living life on my own terms. I invite you to take up residence in my life. I surrender to Your will for my life. I lay all of my sins, including my idols and addictions, at the foot of the cross you died upon. Change me from the inside out and give me new desires that please you. Break my heart with the things that break yours. Stamp eternity upon my eyes. Fill me with your Spirit and help me to live for You each new day. Thank you for your grace and mercy toward me. It's in the glorious name of Jesus I pray, Amen.

Whether you're a new or seasoned believer in Christ, I encourage you to read some of the Bible each day, spend time in prayer, and connect to a local Bible-believing church weekly. These things will help you continue growing in Christ.

DAY 16
Taking Out the Trash

"But if we confess our sins to him, he is faithful and just to forgive us our sins and to cleanse us from all wickedness."
– 1 John 1:9 (NLT)

Once every couple of weeks, my dad would call out to anyone within earshot, "I'm headed to the dump if anyone wants to come with me." In a town of just over 3,000 people, going to the waste transfer station (aka "The Dump") was an adventure.

Getting to the dump involved taking Dole Road which offered beautiful views of our little logging town of Myrtle Creek and some of the Umpqua Valley. Dad would always scare the daylights out of us by seeing how close he could park his 1980 Chevy pickup to the edge of a steep cliff as we viewed the South Umpqua River hundreds of feet below.

After arriving at the dump, dad would back his truck until the tailgate was literally over one of the huge metal trash bins below. And then the dumping would commence. There was something mesmerizing about watching trash and junk fall into the bins. If a bin was completely empty when we arrived, there was the added sound bonus as harder objects like steel, glass, or wood made a loud crash ten feet below.

No trip to the dump was complete without stopping at the 7-Eleven on the way home to get Big Gulps and Slurpees. All that dumping required rehydrating after all!

I'm grateful to have places like waste transfer stations where our accumulated garbage can be taken. I'm also thankful we have a God who allows us to "dump on Him" as our spiritual trash builds.

"But if we confess our sins to him, he is faithful and just to forgive us our sins and to cleanse us from all wickedness." (1 John 1:9 NLT)

Just like my family never had to worry about the waste transfer station returning our garbage to us, neither will Jesus return the sin we bring before him. In fact, he has a wonderful way of somehow making our trash completely disappear as if it never existed. The prophet Micah describes what many have referred to as a "sea of forgetfulness",

"Once again you will have compassion on us. You will trample our sins under your feet and throw them into the depths of the ocean!" (Micah 7:19 NLT)

King David knew all about God's trash removal services…

"He has removed our sins as far from us as the east is from the west." (Psalm 103:12 NLT)

Unlike the Myrtle Creek waste transfer station that had limited hours, God's Sea of Forgetfulness is open 24-7. With our gracious God, there's never a bad time to take out the trash.

Reflection: Have you had some spiritual garbage accumulate in your life? Spend some time confessing to the Lord (dumping) anything weighing you down today and trust that He'll remember it no more.

DAY 17
But God

"But God showed his great love for us by sending Christ to die for us while we were still sinners."
– Romans 5:8 (NLT)

On February 5th, 2017, things looked pretty bleak for the New England Patriots in Super Bowl Fifty-One. By the middle of the third quarter, they found themselves down 28-3 to the Atlanta Falcons. No team had ever come back to win a Super Bowl after such a deficit.

But as can happen in sports across the spectrum, a swing in momentum can change things in a hurry. There would be no Falcons blowout that day. Instead, the Patriots would score thirty-one unanswered points to win the game 34-28 in overtime. As baseball legend Yogi Berra used to say, "It ain't over til it's over."

When it comes to a momentum swing in life, two little words can change the outcome…

But God.

Joseph's brothers intended harm – "but God intended it all for good. He brought me to this position so I could save the lives of many people." (Genesis 50:20 NLT)

David was being pursued by violent people seeking to kill him – "But God is my helper. The Lord keeps me alive!" (Psalm 54:4 NLT)

Jonah was headed toward a grave inside of a whale – "But you, O LORD my God, snatched me from the jaws of death!" (Jonah 2:6b NLT)

Jesus expands our limits – "Jesus looked at them intently and said, "Humanly speaking, it is impossible. But with God everything is possible." (Matthew 19:26 NLT)

Jesus was placed inside a tomb – "But God raised him from the dead!" (Acts 13:30 NLT)

Paul was arrested for preaching the Gospel – "But God has protected me right up to this present time so I can testify to everyone, from the least to the greatest." (Acts 26:22a NLT)

Few if any would die in our place – "But God showed his great love for us by sending Christ to die for us while we were still sinners." (Romans 5:8 NLT)

Like Paul, we face conflict from every direction including internal fear – "But God, who encourages those who are discouraged, encouraged us by the arrival of Titus." (2 Corinthians 7:6 NLT)

We used to follow our own evil desires as rebels toward God – "But God is so rich in mercy, and he loved us so much…" (Ephesians 2:4 NLT)

Paul considered himself the worst of sinners (don't we all?) – "But God had mercy on me so that Christ Jesus could use me as a prime example of his great patience with even the worst sinners." (1 Timothy 1:16a NLT)

Like Israel in Egypt, we've all been a slave to something – "…but the LORD your God brought you out with his strong hand and powerful arm." (Deuteronomy 5:15 NLT)

There will be moments in our lives when the odds seem overwhelmingly against us. Defeat is a foregone conclusion. A comeback? Impossible.

But God.

Reflection: Share a "but God" story with someone you know who could use some encouragement today.

DAY 18
A Crushing Defeat

"The God of peace will soon crush Satan under your feet."
– Romans 16:20a (NLT)

When we hear the words, "crushing defeat", things like lopsided sporting events or political landslides come to mind. Throughout history, we've also been reminded that countries are dealt crushing defeats in war. Needless to say, these types of defeats are overwhelming and decisive.

In Mel Gibson's *The Passion of the Christ*, there's a scene in the Garden of Gethsemane when Jesus is wrestling with the anguish of what awaits him in the hours ahead. It's the same scene we read in Dr. Luke's gospel where "he was in such agony of spirit that his sweat fell to the ground like great drops of blood." (Luke 22:44)

What I like about this scene in the movie is the creative liberty Gibson took by adding a snake slithering up to Jesus while he's praying on his knees. Not at all startled, Jesus calmly stands to his feet before looking at the devil who released the serpent.

The destiny of mankind hangs in the balance. What will Jesus do as he's tempted to avoid the horrors of the cross?

In one swift motion, Jesus crushes the head of the snake with his sandaled heel as if to say, "Nothing is going to deter me from finishing what my Father asked me to do." It's a powerful scene that made me want to jump up in the theater and yell, "TAKE THAT DEVIL!!"

This is the swift action Adam failed to take after being tempted in the first Garden. Humanity (you and I included) has been caving in to the smooth words of the tempter ever since.

But God (remember those words?) had a plan. He didn't just leave us to figure our own way out of the mess. Speaking to the original serpent, God gives us a glimpse of His plans,

"And I will put enmity between you and the woman, and between your offspring and hers; he will crush your head, and you will strike his heel." (Genesis 3:15 NIV)

That would be Jesus crushing the head of the devil by enduring the cross and overcoming death. It's the most crushing defeat of all time that had an eternal ripple effect.

Like the believers in Rome who were enduring trials and persecution, we can also take comfort in these words Paul wrote,

"The God of peace will soon crush Satan under your feet." (Romans 16:20a NLT)

That gets me really excited! Then again, I've never been a fan of snakes…especially the talking kind.

Reflection: Isaiah 53:5 says Jesus was "crushed for our iniquities" or sins. This kind of crushing, like with olives or grapes in a press, leads to something sweet and aromatic. Spend some time thanking Jesus for his willingness to be crushed in order to bring you to eternal victory.

DAY 19
Man on a Mission

"This letter is from Paul, a slave of Christ Jesus, chosen by God to be an apostle and sent out to preach his Good News." – Romans 1:1 (NLT)

I first met Felipe Pena at the end of 1993 while on a two week mission trip to Belize, Central America organized by the college I attended. We were helping to add a kitchen to the church Felipe pastored in a little rural town known as 7 Miles Village.

Pastor Felipe and his family were among many who immigrated to Belize in order to escape the brutal decades-long civil war that took place in their native Guatemala. To this day, there are many small villages scattered around Belize populated by Salvadoran and Guatemalan refugees.

One of the things I admired about Pastor Felipe on that first trip was his willingness to jump in and get his hands and feet dirty. Most rural Latin American men have basic construction skills that include bricklaying, cement work, roofing and flooring. Pastor Felipe is no exception. It's as common to see hm in knee-high rubber boots as it is in his Sunday dress shoes.

During the two years (2002-2004) Shelley and I served as short-term missionaries in Belize, we became very close to Pastor Felipe and his wife Helena. Since then, we've enjoyed supporting the ministry they do throughout this little country of half a million people.

Pastor Felipe's heart and passion has been to plant churches in the poorest villages and to raise up pastors to serve in those settings. This humble man has helped plant dozens of churches across Belize along with helping construct the buildings they gather in.

To give you an example of this man's tireless passion, I remember a season when Felipe drove an old rusted out 1970s Datsun car from village to village on less than ideal roads. When the headlights quit working, did this halt his ministry? Hardly. Instead, he had one of his sons hanging out the passenger side window shining a flashlight on the dark road ahead.

On another occasion, Shelley and I joined Felipe for a ministry excursion to Blue Creek Village located in the southern part of Belize. At nearly four hours' drive, this village of 250 people had no idea we were coming. But like Paul's vision in Acts 16:9 of a man from northern Greece pleading, "Come over to Macedonia and help us!", Felipe sensed the Spirit pleading, "Go down to Blue Creek and help the people there."

Blue Creek is made up of Mayan people who speak the Kekchi language, of which none of us knew a single word. No worries! The Lord led us to a man who could speak some English and Spanish along with his native Kekchi.

Armed with his bible, an old film projector, and some gospel films, Felipe was able to draw a good portion of the village to the town center where they would hear the message of Jesus. It was a fantastic couple days of ministry where multiple barriers were overcome and God was glorified.

Not many outside this little country of Belize will know the name Felipe Pena but I can guarantee Heaven knows his name. And I'm grateful that you can see a glimpse of this man we've grown to love deeply.

This humble servant is a man on a mission like a stealth bomber quietly wreaking havoc upon the kingdom of darkness one remote village at a time.

Reflection: Have you been impacted by someone faithfully serving the Lord quietly in their corner of the world? Let them know how grateful you are for their life today.

Enjoying a cup of Mayan coffee with Pastor Felipe

Pastor Felipe preaching his heart out

DAY 20
This is not my Home

"For this world is not our permanent home; we are looking forward to a home yet to come." – Hebrews 13:14 (NLT)

by Kim Bookmyer

A number of years ago, I went to collect the mail from the box on our porch. You know the routine – flip through some ads, junk mail, maybe a bill, hoping for a personal note of some kind. This time, however, I noticed that there was a piece of mail with a similar address but not our name. 1304. That was our house number but it was a different street and a different name. I grabbed a pen to mark "wrong address" and put it back in the box for our postal carrier to get the next day. It's then when I heard this gentle whisper... Deliver it yourself."

I'd been growing in my ability to recognize the nudging of the Holy Spirit so I seized this as an opportunity to get involved in something God was up to. It was a beautiful day and I had the time right then to walk the few blocks to deliver the mail. I'd like to tell you that I went immediately. But it sat on my desk for a few days. Each time I saw it, I'd think…I really should obey. Finally, I picked it up and left my house, my mind went a number of directions – mostly trying to "talk me out" of taking the piece of mail. I'm so thankful the Lord gave me the courage to obey His voice for I was about to meet someone that God would use to encourage my walk with Him.

Melissa Gertz. She answered the knock on the door with a huge smile and such a welcoming spirit. I told her what had happened with her piece of mail and that began a friendship in Christ that the Lord used to teach me so much.

By knowing Melissa, I learned what it was like to be bold for Jesus. She shared stories of her life and her times in India.

By knowing Melissa, I learned how to lean into Jesus when relationships and circumstances were difficult and how to walk through forgiving others.

By knowing Melissa, I learned about praying and believing for God to do more than we ask or imagine.

By knowing Melissa, I learned how to live for Jesus but also how to die with Jesus. Watching her live out her life during her battle with cancer has taught me so much about realizing that "This is NOT our home!" Our 1304 addresses were our temporary places but our home is in the Presence of Jesus. She made it home sooner than me.

The day Melissa went into hospice, I had a divine opportunity (especially since we moved from Findlay, Ohio over 2 years ago!) to visit with her on her front porch at 1304 one last time – She told me, "Kim, I'll come running to greet you when you arrive but I hope for you to stay here longer and enjoy being a great-grandma someday! Live for Jesus and remember – He's victorious!" And she sent me back to my temporary home with her familiar victory cry and a knowing in my spirit that this life is not all that there is.

Only the Lord knows the number of days we have on this earth, our temporary home.

Reflection: What are others learning about Jesus by knowing me? By knowing you?

This devotion was a guest contribution by our good friend Kim Bookmyer. She is someone who asks the Lord to give her the grace and courage to make her life available to Him. Kim has a Master of Arts in Family Ministry from Winebrenner Seminary in Findlay, OH.

Kim and her husband John reside in Indianapolis, Indiana and have two grown children along with two grandchildren.

DAY 21

When the Meager is Multiplied

"What can I do to help you?" Elisha asked. "Tell me, what do you have in the house?"
- 2 Kings 4:2a (NLT)

Have you ever been in a situation where it was difficult to make ends meet? When there was more month than money? Where the butter was spread way too thin on that slice of bread? Running on fumes and coasting into the gas station is a regular occurrence. And the bills continue coming in like one crashing wave after another against the shores of your life.

That's the scene playing out in the lives of a widow and her two sons (2 Kings 4:1-7). The family breadwinner has died and now a creditor has come knocking on their door to collect. Unable to pay, the only other option is for her boys to work off the debt as slaves. But she knows a man of God in the area. In fact, her husband used to serve alongside this man known as Elisha.

Down to her last thread of hope, the widow shares her predicament with this man who served under and succeeded the great prophet, Elijah.

"What can I do to help you?" Elisha asked.

This simple, open-ended question is one that all of us can ask when we encounter those in need. It's also a question that would have been fresh on Elisha's mind. Just two chapters earlier, his mentor Elijah asked him, "Tell me what I can do for you before I am taken away." (2 Kings 2:9)

Not waiting for the widow's response to this question, Elisha drills down with a more practical question, "Tell me, what do you have in the house?"

Taking a quick inventory, she responds, "Nothing at all, except a flask of olive oil."

You can just see the wheels of faith begin turning in Elisha's head as he tells her to go door to door collecting as many empty jars as she can. Liking this idea better than becoming slaves, the two boys rustled and wrangled every jar in the area.

And then the miraculous flow of oil began. Who knows how many jars were filled from that one meager flask? The oil flow was limited only by the number of empty jars available. Truth be told, those two boys could have scrounged up every jar throughout Israel and the Source wouldn't have run dry.

In the end, this family of three was able to pay off their debts and live off what was left over. Maybe they started a business and called it, "Widow and Sons Olive Oil, LLC."

Whether it's a single flask of olive oil that keeps flowing or five loaves and two fish that keeps feeding, we serve the God who is more than able to meet a particular need.

Jesus will multiply every meager area of our lives if we will simply surrender what little we have in complete obedience.

He's the same yesterday, today, and forever. (Hebrews 13:8)

Reflection: Bring your meager situation before the Lord today. How would you answer if Jesus asked you, "What can I do to help you?" Try to be as specific as possible.

CONCLUSION

One of the things I enjoyed about the trips to Byron, Wyoming where my family would visit grandma and grandpa is the homemade bread grandma would make. The aroma of fresh-baked bread is one of the most intoxicating smells on planet earth. Slathering butter along with grandma's homemade strawberry jam on a slice of warm bread right out of the oven could rival the food of angels.

As tasty as grandma's fresh bread was, the best it could offer was physical nourishment. And as Jesus responded to the devil after being tempted to turn stones into loaves of bread,

'People do not live by bread alone, but by every word that comes from the mouth of God.' (Matthew 4:4b NLT)

The devil's temptation was essentially one of instant gratification. "You know you're hungry Jesus…with a quick command, you can quiet those hunger pangs in your belly with some fresh baked bread."

Jesus wasn't buying it. Even in his fasted state, he was enjoying a feast that went beyond physical satisfaction. His Father and Holy Spirit were supplying a hidden manna straight from the storehouses of heaven.

Today, we're offered a myriad of temptations geared to take the easy route to instant gratification. Things that taste and feel good in the moment but leave us far less satisfied than we had hoped.

In a letter to a church of local believers in Pergamum in northwest Turkey, Jesus offered these hope-filled words in light of the temptations and challenges they faced,

"Anyone with ears to hear must listen to the Spirit and understand what he is saying to the churches. To everyone who is victorious I will give some of the manna that has been hidden away in heaven." (Revelation 2:17a NLT)

These words are just as relevant to those of us in our own local churches. If we refuse the cheap substitutes offered to us by our spiritual enemy, we, too, will be partakers of this 'manna that has been hidden away in heaven.'

The manna Jesus refers to here is a symbol representing Himself. Just as God sustained and strengthened the Israelites with manna during their forty years of wilderness wanderings, Jesus strengthens and sustains

His Church as we journey through this life on our way to heaven.

Just how nourishing is Jesus? We find out through his own words,

"Yes, I am the bread of life! Your ancestors ate manna in the wilderness, but they all died. Anyone who eats the bread from heaven, however, will never die. I am the living bread that came down from heaven. Anyone who eats this bread will live forever; and this bread, which I will offer so the world may live, is my flesh." (John 6:48-51 NLT)

By partaking of the Bread of Life, we are nourished both now and into eternity!

My hope is that we will come to recognize the cheap substitutes the enemy tries to tempt us with and see them as utterly unsatisfying.

May our spiritual taste buds come to crave the nourishment found only in Christ...the true Manna from Heaven.

GET FREE CHRISTIAN BOOKS

Love getting FREE Christian books online? If so, sign up to be notified of new Christian book promotions and never miss out. Then, grab a cup of coffee and enjoy reading the free Christian books you download.

You will also get our FREE report, "How to Find Free Christian Books Online" that shows you 7 places you can get new books for free!

Sign up here: www.bodyandsoulpublishing.com/freebooks

Happy reading!

OTHER BOOKS
BY CJ HITZ

A Heart for Prayer
Encounters with Jesus
Forgiveness Formula
21 Prayers of Generosity
21 Stories of Generosity
21 Days of Generosity Challenge
Unshackled and Free
Fuel for the Soul

And more!

See the entire list here:
www.amazon.com/CJ-Hitz/e/B005KMBT1C

ABOUT CJ HITZ

CJ Hitz and his wife, Shelley, enjoy sharing God's Truth through their speaking engagements and their writing. They enjoy spending time outdoors running, hiking, and exploring God's beautiful creation. CJ and Shelley reside in Colorado Springs, Colorado.

To find out more about CJ and to contact him about speaking at your next event in person or online, send an email to cj@cjhitz.com or find him at www.body-andsoulpublishing.com/about-cj-hitz.

Note from the Author: Reviews are gold to authors! If you have enjoyed this book, would you consider reviewing it on Amazon.com? Thank you!